PSYCHOLOGY OF THE CHILD
IN THE MIDDLE CLASS

Horace Mann Lecture, 1960

PSYCHOLOGY OF THE CHILD
IN THE MIDDLE CLASS

BY

ALLISON DAVIS
Professor of Education
The University of Chicago

PITTSBURGH
UNIVERSITY OF PITTSBURGH PRESS
1960

TO

RALPH W. TYLER and FRANCIS S. CHASE

Educators With A Faith
In
The Social Sciences

HORACE MANN LECTURES

THE HORACE MANN
LECTURESHIP

To commemorate the life of Horace Mann, 1796-1859, and in recognition of his matchless services to the American Public School System, the School of Education of the University of Pittsburgh, in cooperation with the Tri-State Area School Study Council, established the Horace Mann Lectureship. The striking and varied Contributions of Horace Mann must ever be kept alive and be re-emphasized in each generation. It is difficult, indeed, to assess the magnitude of Mann's educational services. Turning from the profession of law he devoted his life to the study and improvement of education. He, more than any other, can truly be called "Father of the American Public School System." His boundless energy, coupled with a brilliant and penetrating mind, focused the attention of the citizens of his era on the need for the improvement and sup-

PORT OF PUBLIC SCHOOLS. HIS SERVICES
WERE MANIFOLD. IT SHALL BE THE PUR-
POSE OF THESE LECTURES TO RE-AFFIRM
HIS FAITH IN FREE SCHOOLS AND TO CALL
TO THEIR SERVICE ALL CITIZENS OF THIS
GENERATION. IT IS VITAL THAT ALL UN-
DERSTAND THE PURPOSE AND FUNCTION
OF A FREE PUBLIC SCHOOL SYSTEM IN
AMERICAN DEMOCRACY.

THE HORACE MANN LECTURES ARE PUB-
LISHED ANNUALLY BY THE UNIVERSITY
OF PITTSBURGH PRESS.

PSYCHOLOGY OF THE CHILD
IN THE MIDDLE CLASS

I

It is a hot summer's day, and my office is not air-conditioned. A man in overalls stands on a steel girder outside my window, grasping a riveting machine. He is helping erect the framework of a new university building. He is also creating a brain-shattering clatter. No doubt he is a very friendly man personally, and a useful one. Certainly there are skills involved in his work, although I do not know what they are. But it has got to the point where one of us has to leave, and I feel it should be the riveter. He could learn his skills in a few months or years, I tell myself, whereas it took me much longer. At the moment I feel I could do without him and his skills which seem much less valuable than mine. Yet I am fairly certain, having known such working men, that he feels the same way about professors and is convinced of the greater value of his skills as compared to theirs. He may be correct, but society and especially middle-class people are determined to make their children into professional men rather than riveters.

Such differences in the evaluation of occupations may be personal, but they are more likely to be taught by our modern social system. Even in Russia, the professor, the engineer, and the surgeon are regarded by the total society as more important than the riveter. In other words, a social class system has developed. In our country, a person must have had about sixteen years of education to become an engineer, nineteen or twenty years to become a professor, and about twenty-five years to become a surgeon or specialist in medicine. Most children in the middle class today will complete college, and most of the upper middle-class boys will become professional men or business executives. Their parents and teachers are acutely aware of the long education required for these positions. As standards rise and competition increases, nearly every middle-class parent sets the goals higher for his children and increases the pressure for achievement.

What is the process of rearing and educating children and adolescents so that they may be capable of assuming the most complex intellectual and moral responsibilities in our society? What are the social relationships involved in this process, and what are the emotional problems to be solved by the child? The society seems to demand only that it have enough well-trained physicists, mathematicians, administrators, technicians, teachers, engineers, statesmen and diplomats, and not to be mindful of the cost of the training in terms of the emotional and ego resources of the individual. Yet the rate of mental illness, alcoholism, and other personality disorders among middle-class people has been and remains so high as to make it clear that this highly competitive way of life, to which middle-class people themselves often refer as "the rat race," can be maintained successfully only by those who have both the training and the personalities for it. Big business seems to be learning this truth, and it is time that parents and teachers considered it very seriously with children. In this essay, we shall direct our attention, therefore, to some of the processes in the emotional development of the child in the middle class. We shall then consider the relationship of these emotional processes to (1) failure or achievement in a career and to (2) a sense of personal identity and autonomy.

There are two concepts which inevitably recur in the study of the personality development of the child in the middle class. They are *status* and *achievement*. Status will be defined later in this essay. Here it is sufficient to say that one may speak of the status of father and the status of son; the father is superordinate in power and authority, the son is subordinate. One may also speak of the status of brothers; their status with respect to each other is coordinate or equivalent in our society. One may also speak of the status of the upper class, the middle class, and the lower class, which would be respectively, the top, the middle, and the bottom of the hierarchy of social strata. All children, no matter what their social-class origin, or country,

are subordinate within the family to
their parents, and also to other adults in
the age-privilege hierarchy.

The concept of achievement is central
in the psychology of middle-class individuals for the following reasons: (1)
Unlike individuals in the "leisure class,"
or aristocracy, who inherit their positions of distinction in both the social and
financial worlds, the middle-class individual usually has to achieve his position
in the manufacturing or business world,
and always must achieve it in the professional world. He must strive toward
the attainment of long-postponed goals,
and compete effectively with others who
are similarly striving; (2) this striving
reaches the point of powerful and some-
times destructive aggression in the business and political worlds, where "competition" generally ignores the rules of
middle-class morality as taught to the
child; this competitive aggression is becoming more typical, furthermore, of the
professional world as the number of
those competing increases; (3) this competitive drive for achievement is learned

by the child in his family and school, which seek in the middle class to convert the child's aggression into socially directed initiative and striving for achievement. As will be indicated later in this essay, the child's aggression is transformed into striving for achievement by the processes of (1) identification with the parent, involving anxiety, and of (2) exploiting the ego-goals actually available to his age-status in the family, playgroup, and school. Thus, the question of the channeling and transformation of aggression in the middle-class child will be one of the principal concerns of this essay. The importance of this area for the middle-class individual is further indicated by the experience of psychiatrists who find that in the American middle-class the basic emotional problems of those who feel they have failed at life are often problems of the excessively high level of achievement and social mobility which the individual has sought, and which in some cases the parents may have set for him.

II

With the concepts of status and achievement in mind, this essay will proceed along the following course. First, status will be defined and illustrated. Then the psychological processes involved in status in the family, in the age-groups, and in relationships between males and females will be traced. Finally, the psychology of the middle-class child who is directed toward upward social mobility will be considered.

"Status," like any other highly abstract term, such as "electricity" or "heat" or "energy," can have little meaning until the processes to which it refers have been described. Status will be defined here as a certain kind of human relationship, and the emotional responses of children in status-relationships will be described.

Status is a social relationship. A social relationship consists of mutual interaction between two or more human beings. This interaction is such that the behavior and emotions of each party to the relationship are influenced by the behavior and emotions of the other party or parties. Thus in the husband-wife relationship, the behavior of the husband leads to a certain range of responses by the wife. If the husband is aggressive toward the wife, she may respond with counter-aggression, or with subservience, or with an effort to come to an understanding of his aggression. Whatever course she follows, she will influence his subsequent behavior. If she is aggressive, she may increase his aggression thereby, or she may battle him on equal terms, or she may frighten him. Thus the action and feeling of each party influences the action and feeling of the other in every type of situation. Whether they realize it or not, they are interdependent. If the wife waits on the husband, he may take advantage of this service as his right, or he may refuse it, or he may try to return it by waiting on her in some way. In any event, she will be influenced by his acts, either by being confirmed in her habit of waiting on him, or by feeling rejected, or by learning to expect a return service from him.

Any interaction between two people is a relationship. A *social* relationship, however, is an interaction which is influenced by cultural teachings or models, and in which there takes place some *compromise* or *adjustment* between the drives or desires of two or more people. It is this adjustment or conciliation of the drives of the parties involved which makes the interaction "social." Even a fight between two people has the character of a social relationship, provided there are some recognized or cultural rules to govern the conditions of the conflict. In such a fight, the rage and aggression of each party have to be modified to conform to the limits set by the group, as in the case of two boys who must "fight fair," i.e., according to the rules of the gang.

Status, then, is a social relationship. It is a relationship in which the social rank and privileges of the parties involved are culturally defined as *unequal*. It is a relationship in which one member is regarded by the other, and regards himself, as socially superordinate, whereas the second member is regarded by the first, and regards himself, as subordinate. The rank of each is defined by the culture.

The concept of status, or of a particular status, always includes in this essay both the concept of a *role*, such as that of *son* to father, and the concept of the *rank* accorded socially to this role (the son, as a child, is *subordinate* to the father). That is, each status has a culture and a rank. The culture, learned in the family, play-group, school, church, and other groups, defines the behavior and emotions proper to a given role. The particular social group defines the rank of this role in relation to other roles.

Culture, in the sense meant here, is of course a psychological system, since it exists within individuals and is composed of the thoughts, concepts of right and wrong, concepts of appropriate roles, etc., which individuals have learned from and share with their social groups. Properly speaking, there is no difference in *kind* between a psychological system and a cultural system of relationships. Both systems consist of similar kinds of internal behavior of men; of perceptions, memories, acts of cognition, of generalizations, and so on. Any cultural system of human relationships is, in the final analysis, a psychological system; the acts which compose it are psychic acts which have been learned in conformity with a group.

Thus culture is composed of certain types of psychological systems within individuals, namely those systems which have to do with learning the behavior of social groups. To be more exact, culture may be said to consist of a class of similar psychological systems existing in many individuals. This class of cultural psychological systems is distinguished from other psychological systems by the characteristic that it includes only that behavior which is learned from and approved by a social group.

The preceding definition of status as a "social relationship in which the rank and privileges of the parties involved are culturally defined as unequal" will, as was predicted at the beginning of this essay, have little meaning until the human processes involved are described. One cannot see status. Indeed in our country we seldom see even the symbols of status, such as exist in a nobility with its titles and court dress, or in the special way in which a girl's hair used to be arranged in contrast to the coiffure of a woman, or in the short pants which boys once wore to distinguish their dress from that of men. In fact, we seem not to be able to recognize powerful status systems which exist under our very eyes, and which determine a great deal of the behavior of our children and of ourselves. No doubt it is owing to the fact that we are adults, and therefore at the top of the system of age-status, that we are unable to perceive clearly the powerful restrictions which this system places upon children and adolescents, and the emotional demands it makes of them. We are not under the hammer and therefore do not feel its power.

In order to realize what status means and how it may affect human behavior, perhaps one should recall his own adoles-

cence. Then, as now, the adolescent was
socially limited in most of the basic areas
of human development. He is especially
limited in the middle-class culture. He
has to live with his parents, and he is
in the position of an economic dependent
with respect to his food, his clothes, his
schooling, his shelter, his medical care.
In Chicago and many cities, he is legally
or by custom restricted, owing to his age,
from working. His sexual maturity and
independence are discouraged by most
parents in the middle class, and by the
punishments of the total society. Even
when this is not the case, his sexual life
is inhibited or conflicted by his economic
and social dependence upon his parents;
to gain a full sense of sexual identity
and rights he needs an occupation and
a home of his own. In high school he
is treated like a child, subjected to many
of the same types of discipline used in
elementary schools, and given very few
opportunities to develop in adult roles
and to think of himself as becoming independent.

Yet our society is mystified and full of anxiety about its adolescents! Parents, teachers, politicians, and social workers cannot understand what is wrong with this generation, or any other generation, of adolescents. Psychologists assume that the confusion, lack of confidence, and chronic hostility toward adults which adolescents feel are inevitable at their age. While it is true that the adolescent has certain emotional problems with respect to his sexual and aggressive desires, these are emotions which he could learn to control by the time he is sixteen or seventeen, if he had the social permission to work and live as an adult. People of this age in other types of societies, which have been studied by anthropologists, do not exhibit the childishness, the confusion about their present and future place in society, or the hostility, which are typical of adolescents in our society.

The major trouble with adolescents in our society is that we keep them in the status of children in most areas of their lives. The adult society, as represented by the parents, the school, and the occu-

pational structure, will not permit the
middle-class adolescent, although he is
physiologically a man or woman, to have
an occupation, to be economically independent, to live in a home of his own,
or to marry. A great part of adolescent
"diffusion" and disorganization must result from this powerful social blocking
of the adolescent's drives for independence.

The adolescent understands what is
meant by a status system. Wherever the
adolescent turns in the effort to gain def-
initeness, competence, and autonomy as
a man or woman, he is systematically
blocked by our society (except, possibly,
in lower-lower class). He cannot develop
his abilities in any of the major areas of
social and economic life, because those
areas are preempted by adults and for-
bidden to him. In those societies which
permit their adolescents to work, to
marry, and to establish a home of their
own, this same age-group shows little
of the neurotic and childish behavior
found in most of our adolescents (or in
most of us when we were adolescent).

We have a very deeply ingrained and very powerful status system in which adults are superordinate and the adolescent age-group is very subordinate. But when we try to understand, or teach, or help our adolescents, we forget or ignore the fact that society is keeping them childish, and that their basic ego-drives are blocked in a way that is certain to make them confused or hostile or bored or hopeless.

In this essay the attempt will be made to examine several kinds of social status systems, and especially to trace the psychological and emotional effects of superior and inferior status upon the individual. Most Americans writing on social status miss the most important finding of sociologists and anthropologists concerning status in human society. This is the fact that status of some type exists in every human society, and that it has always existed in many different forms in American society.

We Americans may still have unpleasant feelings when we hear the term, "social class," used in a description of one of our basic status systems. We are even more uncomfortable, as Gunnar Myrdal has pointed out in *The American Dilemma,* when we think of the color-status system which exists in our country. These concepts and the social facts to which they refer are in conflict with both our democratic ideals and our religious teachings. One does not know how this social, moral, and emotional conflict will be resolved. One doubts very much that any of these systems of status will disappear, but one believes they will be modified in such a way that the conflicting interests of the different groups will be adjusted for a period, after which new conflict and dissatisfaction will mount, and a new modification be necessary.

This emotional process of conflict and its resolution underlies all social relationships. All status systems are maintained by a precarious balance in which each party to the relationship makes certain gains and accepts certain losses. When one party to the status-relationship feels that his losses outweigh his gains from the system, the old status system will no

longer operate, but a new one is invari-
ably developed. In the case of the status
system of adolescents and adults, time
breaks up the system. The adolescent
becomes a man or woman— the equal of
his parents and other adults. Neverthe-
less, the social and cultural *principle* of
age-status remains in effect in the society, so that adolescents are subordinate
to adults in each generation.

Like all complex societies, that of the
United States includes a vast number of
status systems. We have status within
segments of our society such as schools,
churches, factories, law-courts, political
parties, government, the armed services,
civic and social organizations, and many
other institutions. We have also the
broader status systems of social classes,
ethnic groups and color-groups, into
which a person is born. But, psychologically, the most powerful systems of status in our society and in practically all
human societies are the family, the age-
groups, and the sex-groups. It is true,
therefore, that status has been a lifelong
reality in the lives of all of us. Further-

more, each of us has been *subordinate* to
others, not only in the class system, but
also in the family and in the age groups;
each of us also has been *superordinate* to
someone or to some group. Psychologically, one of the most powerful reinforcements of status systems is the fact that
everyone in the system is likely to be
socially defined as superior to someone,
and thus to gain some prestige from the
system.

Status may be formally designated in
a group by titles and offices, as in the
army, or church, or a business firm, or
status may be informally defined by culture and tradition as in a social class or
family. Some of the most intimate and
informal human relationships involve
status. In fact, at the heart of the social
relationship between parent and child,
or older sibling and younger sibling,
there lies the emotional and social reality
we call status.

The child learns in his own family his
basic social and emotional pattern of re-
sponse to status positions, to superordi-
nates, to subordinates, and to peers. The

parents, even those who have extremely "permissive" attitudes, cannot fail to reveal to the child their superior strength, power, and status. They not only control money, and therefore food, clothing, and other such necessities, but they also control the child's range of behavior, and his access to some of the gratifications he seeks. They possess and control each other, as the child cannot. They bring other children into the family to replace him or to take away part of the attention he receives. They determine the major pleasures and disappointments in his life.

The family thus provides the child and the adult with both his concept of, and his feelings about status. The family is the basic model and archetype of social-status relationships of all three types, viz., inferior, equal, and superior. In the family the basic emotions associated with status are also learned, namely, fear, mastery, dependence, hostility, intimacy, and conciliation. Psychiatry teaches us that family life imprints deeply within the child his life-long tendency to accept or to resent those of higher status, to reject or to compete with his peers, to exploit or to share with his inferiors in age. The family is really a hierarchy, with parents occupying the superior status and children the inferior. Our next concern in this essay is to gain some insight into the processes by which the child and the parent deal with the emotional conflicts aroused by this status system.

III

We know from sociological and from clinical research that relationships of differential rank and privilege arouse mutual hostility between individuals who have unequal privileges. This hostility exists even in the young child. The hostility hides the fear which the child feels toward the parent; it is a defensive reaction against his sense of helplessness in the face of derogation or punishment. The child, like any human being, also feels that he has a right to seek pleasure. He has a stake, that is, in the family life, and he wants to attain it, or to defend it. When he is controlled by the parent and denied the pleasures which he seeks, he is frightened by the prospect that any and all of his pleasures may be taken away. This anxiety, which is the anticipation of further criticism and attack, arouses his hostility, his wish to counter-attack, even though his sense of reality tells him that attack would be hopeless.

This hostility, as in all status-relationships, may take one of four courses. (1) It may be expressed, within limits, as chronic aggression toward the parents. This course only increases the child's guilt feelings and anxiety. (2) The hostility toward the parents may be displaced onto siblings. (3) The child's hostility may be repressed and do its destructive work in the creation of irrational anxiety. Or (4) the child's hostility may be transformed, or at least reduced to a tolerable level, through identification with, and reconciliation to, his age-status. The child identifies with the child-group and child-status, as a means of both gaining substitutive gratifications and of controlling and reducing his anxiety and hostility. Within his age-status, within his identity as a "child" he may, as Professor Robert D. Hess has pointed out, also find culturally approved means of developing his initiative and competence. Accepting the identity of his status, he may work within it to make himself less vulnerable to attacks upon his ego both from inside himself and from the outside world.

The hostility is never completely resolved, however. For the privileges and deprivations, both of parent and of child, chronically arouse hostility and stimulate the anticipation of counterhostility by the other party to the status-relationship. This counterhostility moves either "up" or "down" in the status system. We have seen how the child's is aroused. To the parent, himself, the evidence of his child's hostility imply that the parent is not fulfilling the cultural expectations of a "good parent." The child's hostility is a threat to the parent's self-esteem, therefore, and arouses the parent's anxiety and stimulates his counterhostility toward the child.

At the same time a protective, anxiety-reducing process develops in the parent-child relationship. It includes not only the process called "identification." The total process by which the child's anxiety and hostility are reduced involves a reconciliation both on the side of the child and on that of the parent. The culturally "good" child and "good" parent have made a (temporary) peace between them such that the anxiety and hostility of each, which are chronically aroused by the system of status, are reduced. This reconciliation consists in accepting the cultural identity of one's age-status, with its losses as well as its gains. After a long battle and much renunciation, the child accepts, or is reconciled to, the rights and duties and ego-ideals of a "child" as his best available way of life. The parent is reconciled to his responsibilities also. He learns the cultural identity of a "parent," which permits him authority but requires that he accept also the restrictions, duties, and the impulse-renunciations of parenthood. When he can control himself, and accept the cultural injunction to train the child and teach him self-control and responsibility, the parent has embraced the cultural identity of a "parent," which is one side of the social control that makes "peace" —or something, shall we say, different at least from open warfare—between the parent and the child.

To summarize: The young child seeks, first of all, to satisfy his own impulses and reduce his tensions. When his parents or siblings block his pursuit of food, activity, and love, he feels angry. He soon learns that his physical weakness prevents his attacking the parents. As he grows older, he also is deterred from aggression toward the parents by his learned feelings of guilt and anxiety as well as by his desire for approval (identification). But the fact that the parents must deny him many things he wants, together with the basic status structure of privileges inherent in the social structure of the parent-child relationship, still chronically arouses the hostility of the child toward the parent.

The resolution of this hostility is a complex process. Until the child has worked out, through his culturally permitted roles, socially effective forms of initiative and aggression, he has one of two choices. He may either displace his rage from the all-powerful father or mother to a sibling, or he may turn his hostility inward and attack and depreciate himself (as he feels his parents would if they were aware of his resentment toward them). Thus the healthy child expresses his hostility toward his parents by displacing it to his brother or sister. In this way he seeks to preserve his self-regard by counterattacking but, at the same time, saves himself the destructive guilt and anxiety which would be aroused by direct and conscious hostility toward the parents. The other recourses, that is, to repress his hostility, or to attack the parents themselves, or to turn his rage against himself, usually lead to destructive levels of guilt and anxiety.

The methods by which the child handles his aggression are extremely complex. They vary, moreover, from one type of personality to another. Boys may repress their hostility toward the parents, usually the father, and, owing to the repressed hate, become the victims of a great deal of vague anxiety and guilt. Other boys may experience their hostility toward the father at a more nearly conscious level and express it overtly. Still another type of child may develop a deep feeling of rejection and self-depreciation in his early relationships with the parents. Throughout the remainder of his life, he may be seeking to gain continually increasing power, applause, and prestige in an effort to satisfy his insatiable desire to be reassured.

Similarly, one may distinguish several levels of aggression which are developed in the individual's early relationships with his siblings. The normal adaptation, as has been said, is to be jealous of the sibling; every child apparently wants all of his mother's and father's love, or certainly the best part of it. To be jealous of, and to be competitive with, the siblings are therefore almost universal experiences. This rivalry, however, has certain normal limits. It becomes abnormal when the child is obsessed with the feeling that the brother or sister has all the best of it; that he, himself, is rejected by the mother and father. Such a child devotes his life, so to speak, to the self-pity and the feeling of rejection which results from his belief that his sibling has been strongly preferred. Or the reaction may be one of chronic and inextinguishable rage and resentment. The third type of relationship to the sibling is that of overidentification with the sibling. In this case the child apparently feels that the effort to compete with the sibling is hopeless, owing either to the belief that the mother or father has given all his love to the sibling or to the belief that the sibling, himself, is far more able and effective. Such an overidentified individual then feels, apparently, "The best recourse I have is to be just like my brother or sister, to become another one such as he or she." This process by which a sibling loses his identity and initiative in order to escape the resentment of the parent is a most destructive process to the ego. (It is similar to over-identification with a parent and to "identification with the aggressor.")

IV

Age-subordination, which most individuals in our society must learn to accept in economic and social relationships until relatively late in life, theoretically would appear an especially difficult adaptation for the first, or only, child to make. During the first eighteen months of life, a child in any birth-position appears to accept the mother as omnipotent and to depend upon her almost entirely for his biological and emotional nurture. When feeding, cleanliness, and other types of training are required of the infant of this age, they must necessarily be instilled and maintained without the aid of prestige motivation. At the very early age in our society when most infants are required to attempt such learning, the age-prestige motivation of "acting like a big boy or girl" or "acting like Daddy or Mother" cannot yet be effective. As they grow older, however, children with siblings near them in age have constantly before them the goal of the older siblings' behavior to pace them in learning the appropriate age-sex behavior. The only child, the first child, or a child separated by about six years from his nearest sibling, on the other hand, has to face a tremendously steep age-barrier. In most instances, the only or first child is stimulated to strive for adult privileges. Since the only child has no siblings to break the impact of parental stimulation, nor to serve as therapeutic targets for aggression displaced from the parents, his goals are often set by himself or his parents too near the adult level.

A child in this position and family-type also faces added pressure to achieve, for he is the class banner-carrier of the family in the next generation. If in addition, the family is attempting to increase its status in the class system, the first or only child is most likely to be over-pressed. At the opposite pole is the child who, owing either to indulgence or to excessive parental dominance, does not strive for the increasingly complex age-typed behaviors. One result of such extreme parental love-demands or of over-protection is to intensify the age-subordination of the child, and to fix lifelong

marks of child-status upon his behavior.
This consequence seems more likely if
the child in question has no siblings near
his own age from whom he obtains pres-
tige-responses.

Competition for the parents' favor and
care (which is the essential factor in
rivalry between children in the same
family) likewise is expressed through
the system of age-privileges. Each sibling has a stake to defend in this strug-
gle and therefore has a real source of
anxiety. To "beat the game" of age-
privileges with one's siblings is to win
evidence of parental favor, of acceptance
or protection greater than one's age-role
permits. In lower-class families, such
competition appears to be moderated by
the custom of entrusting the parental
role to an older child. Usually each child
thus receives his turn to act as parent-
surrogate to a younger child.

A weak form of this hostility-reducing
relation exists as a device in middle-and
upper-class families, by which the older
sibling is allowed to assume minor care

and supervision of a younger sibling, or is told, "This is your baby."

The problem of securing to the child in our society an adequate level of aggression for later adult life appears to center in the early management of age roles and privileges in his relationship to parents and siblings. As the child moves upward in the age-hierarchy, both his social clique and school, as well as his familial relationships, define the appropriate age-behaviors and evaluations. These family, clique, and school roles are psychologically maintained by sanctions which instigate the child toward the allowed prestige goals, and penalize inappropriate age-participation. Within the family, biosocial and psychosocial privileges such as food and sweets, clothes, a room to one's self, an allowance, lunch money, courting and sexual exploration, use of the automobile, etc., are age-typed. Forms of play are likewise age-graded by both the family and the child's clique.

The school is our most thoroughly age-graded institution. With compulsory promotion still operating in many public

school systems, we have a form of auto-
matic, involuntary age-grading which
has had few parallels in primitive societies. In the social life of the elementary
or secondary school pupil, great differen-
tiation in rank and clique behavior exists
between groups separated by only one or
two age-grades.

Probably as a result of the history of
their identification with, and competition
for the parents, children differ with respect to their adaptation to the age-hierarchy of the family and larger society.
Some accept the required role, others
strive vigorously for the privileges of a
higher age-group, and still others flee
downward from the appropriate age-
demands to an earlier level. The child
who pushes hard against the system of
age-rank, fighting by cunning and aggression for the privileges of older siblings or parents is likely to meet especial
difficulty in the adolescent period. At this
time, when he is maturing very rapidly
in sexual and physical status, he excessively resists the subadult status which
society fixes upon him by economic, sex-

ual, and educational subordination. When such upward age-striving children are also basically aggressive toward a parent, they would be expected to rebel fiercely against subadult status in adolescence. Individuals of this type are probably more likely, than are those who either accept or flee downward from their age-status, to strive also for participation with a social class higher than that of their parents. In this upward class-striving, they can subordinate the parent by acquiring etiquette, or educational and occupational symbols which the society recognizes as superior to those of the parents.

V

A second kind of ranked status which the child must learn to accept is the status-identity of a boy or of a girl. The derogation of feminine status and the early intimidation of the girl are general in both European and oriental cultures. It seems clear, also, that in early life, girls in the United States are more severly trained than boys and more systematically intimidated with respect to nearly all the basic psychological drives. Anyone who thinks realistically about the status of women in America will recognize that women are placed at a great status-disadvantage in the economic and political systems and that within the family, itself, the division of labor, privileges, and authority strikingly favors the man—the opinions of European observers notwithstanding.

In fact, the differential status of men and women is a system of rank which, unlike that of parent and child, persists throughout the life of the individual. This lifelong inferiority of the female's status, in spite of her equal, or possibly greater, intellectual capacity, is of course a cultural attack upon the ego of females. Like human beings of any group and every age-level, women respond to this cultural intimidation with anxiety, and then with hostility and guilt. This hostility is directed toward males and also toward the mother who puts into effect the restrictions demanded by the male-dominated society.

We know very little about the psychology of women. Psychologists, male or female, are blinded in their studies of the personality of women by an ethnocentrism which prevents our seeing clearly the powerful status system to which the woman has to reconcile herself.

This reconciliation really means, of course, reconciliation to males, to the father, to the brother, to the husband, to the son. It takes place through the girl's learning to identify with the feminine culture and status. This identity includes the culturally approved but nondominant behavior of tenderness and mothering and personal service to children and husband, as well as the cultural symbolization of the family's class-status, and also a certain amount of sabotage tolerated by the system.

In the normal female personality, the woman has identified with, and committed herself emotionally to, the female status. In this process of status-identification, most of her hostility toward men is resolved, but never all of it. She is reconciled to the feminine status, however, first by its opportunities for positive achievement in the roles of wife and mother, and, second, by the feelings of acceptance, ease, and intimacy which she gets from her own status-group, that of women.

Sex-typing of behavior and privileges is far more rigid and lasting in our society than is age-typing. Indeed, sexual status and color-caste status are the only lifelong forms of rank. In our society, one can escape them in approved fashion only by death. Sex-inappropriate behavior, social or physical, is still one of the most severely punished infractions of our social code.

In most familial, occupational, and political structures the male is trained for the superordinate roles while the female is restricted largely to subordinate positions. As in other types of inferior social rankings, however, the female position allows a certain degree of chronic aggression, sabotage, and cleverness against the superior rank. The modes of expressing personality traits such as fear, aggression, and affection are also socially typed for sex. The sexual role and personality are trained by the family and school, through their insistence upon sex-appropriate language, clothes, hairdress, gait, pitch and intonation of voice, play, recreation, and work. For most of these sex-appropriate behaviors there is certainly no biological basis of sex-linked traits.

There is evidence in clinical and exploratory studies of children to suggest that the child's imitation of a sex-role is functionally related to (1) his early genital training, (2) his learning of the out-marriage rule of the family, and (3) the relative strength of his cross-sex and same-sex identifications with parents. It is certain, however, that in middle-class child-training the sexual impulses are still implicitly tabooed. The degree of severity or abruptness in parental controlling of the sexual impulses seems partly to determine the child's adjustment to the sex-role.

This penalizing of the sex drive itself is intensified in those families where the child is pressed to assume the appropriate sex-role too early or too completely. Parents who are anxious concerning their own sex-typing are likely to overemphasize those controls upon the child. The learning of sex-appropriate behavior also depends upon whether the child's imitation of the same-sex parent is motivated by the effort to escape constant punishment and disfavor, or by positive reinforcements of acceptance and prestige. If he fails to imitate more fully the same-sex parent, owing either (1) to that parent's failure to control and to reward him, or (2) to the cross-sex parent's greater power, the child is likely to reveal the marks of inappropriate sextyping.

The sexual role, which is first defined
by the early family training of the child,
is in successful cases greatly strength-
ened by the sex-typing controls to which
he is subjected later. In his social clique,
his school, and his formal organizations,
the child gains prestige if he learns the
sex-appropriate code, behavior, and
goals, but meets extreme social—and at
times physical—punishment if he does
not. Sexual segregation is not only maintained in most kinds of play until full
adolescence, but also in the school and
church in lower-class environments. In
America as in most societies, the crucial
definition of the sex-appropriate role is
made at adolescence.

VI

The child and adolescent in our society are socialized, then, within a series of personal relationships characterized by rank. These hierarchical relations include, among many others, those between parent or parent-surrogates and child, between teacher and child, and between children, themselves, of different ages and sexes. Thus, the early socialization of the American child occurs largely in relationships where he is subordinated upon the hierarchical principles of inferiority in age, skill, or experience. These relationships of rank, whether between father and son, teacher and pupil, middle-class individual and lower-class individual, are maintained apparently by socially typed motivations and goals which lead the individual to strive for those behaviors which are considered *proper to his status*. In the normal range of personalities, this striving is maintained, it appears, by adaptive forms of socially inculcated and approved anxiety. The intensive study of normal personalities leads inevitably to the recognition of the tremendously vital role of this type of socialized anxiety in the integration and direction of the personality, notably in the development of individuals of middle status.

Essential to effective socialization in our society is the maintenance by the individual of a certain level of anxiety with regard to the attainment of the required behavior for his status. This socialized anxiety plays a major role in propelling him along that cultural route prescribed by his family, school, and later by adult society at his cultural level. The development of adaptive anxiety in middle-status life is all the more essential because the social and prestige rewards of this status must necessarily be postponed during the prolonged training of the child and adolescent for high skills and complex responsibilities. In the meantime, anxiety which threatens the individual with the loss of both present status and of future gains must serve as the basic drive in his socialization.

In all cultural levels in our society, socialized anxiety is a powerful drive. It

is derived from a long and complex series
of training situations in which threats
of social punishment or withdrawal of
approval have been invoked. Since any
of these techniques implies to the child
the loss of his parents' favor or approval
(which in turn is associated with food,
shelter, money, opportunity to study for
a profession, etc.), they all arouse in him
the anticipation of loss, if the expected
behavior is not learned. As the middle-
class child comes into the status of an
adolescent, the level of his socially stimulated anxiety becomes higher, for the
pressure exerted upon him by his parents, social clique, and teachers for attainment in respect to school and preparation for a career, becomes greater.

The foregoing changes in social behavior and goals are maintained partly
by the anxiety to avoid social punishment
and partly by the drive to attain the rewards of social prestige. Anxiety of this
type, therefore, is a most effective motivation toward social learning because it
leads to reward. In middle-class society,
the instrumental acts to attain prestige-

rewards are acts of striving. Thus, anxiety is mobilized not only by the anticipation of punishment if the required behavior is not learned, but by the desire *not* to be *deprived* of reward. It is this striving for reward, for status, *this uneasiness lest the reward be not attained,* which constitutes the adaptive social function of anxiety. Children with strongly developed social anxiety, therefore, usually strive for the approved social goals most eagerly and learn most successfully. In this sense the most fully socialized individuals are those with the most effective, controlled, socially directed anxiety. Freud would be a classic instance of such a person, both as a student and as a leader in research. He was anxious to attain, to excel—and to win his father's approval, which had been denied him, he felt, as a child.

An intensive study of the life histories of normal children and adolescents in our society makes it clear that the behavioral manifestations which teachers and psychologists would regard as "anxious" are often associated with striving behavior. Socially realistic anxiety leads to striving because only thus can anxiety be reduced to a tolerable level. Thus, it may be said that, in our kind of society, if a child wishes to be rewarded, he must learn to mobilize and to bear that degree of anxiety which will serve to make him strive most effectively for the goals of his group.

Middle-class people maintain, organize, and administer American life. The "small people" in the middle group are the backbone of our society; the "upper middles" are the brain and the eyes of the society. Almost all of the good things in American life, as we in education evaluate it, are the achievements of the middle-status persons: care of and pride in property, careful child-training with emphasis upon renunciation and sacrifice for future gains, long and arduous education, development of complex and demanding skills, working and learning one's way up in the complicated processes of business, industry, government, and education—all of them administered (but not controlled) by the upper-middle class in the American status system.

The culture of the middle-status group, as analyzed by observers, is found to be highly institutionalized; the church, the organizations, the school, the formal associations of all types are the basic integrating structures in their society. Along with this highly organized structure goes a marked emphasis upon attaining. As compared to both the lower- and higher-status levels, then, the middle group is more highly organized and its members are more deeply motivated—by all institutions in middle-class—to achieve.

This cultural emphasis upon achievement arises largely from social insecurity: in lower-middle groups it arises largely from the fear of loss of occupation of respectability, which would plunge the family into lower-class life; in upper-middle groups, from the fact that, unlike upper-class people, upper-middles are not born to highest status, but must achieve it in the face of social stigmas and punishment, if it is to be theirs.

The middle-class way, then, with its emphasis upon respectability and morality, upon property, money, and other symbols of attainment, upon organizational ties which dramatize one's adherence to group goals, upon self-improvement through education (or book clubs, or art and music clubs), and upon community improvement through the church, the civic organizations, and the school (a way of life which is obnoxious to Bohemians, aristocrats, and slum dwellers) is carried on by people who are culturally motivated to work and to renounce or postpone gratifications in order to achieve. To propel the child along this apparently endless route of socialization—so that he may attain a physician's skills, let us say—the middle-status family uses pressures and goals which build anxiety. The child is taught by a well-defined and relatively severe training to strive for the expected or allowed age, sex, or class status, or to attempt to gain a higher age, or school, or social-class status. As the child goes through adolescence, furthermore, he is gradually inducted by parents, teachers, and age-mates into the adult pattern of class behavior. Near the end of high school or at the beginning of his college career, he is urged to begin serious study and preparation for an occupation which will maintain the family's status or improve it. A girl is oriented toward either a "decent," "good," or "brilliant" marriage or a skilled or professional occupation.

It seems clear that the sustained striving and the difficult habits of impulse control and organic deprivation which these long educational and socializing processes require (such as the loss of sleep, relaxation, and perhaps of adequate food upon the part of the graduate or medical student who is largely dependent upon his own earnings) are motivated by the adaptive anxiety established by the individual's previous family, school, and status-relationships. To win the mother's approval or the teacher's praise or to win prestige in the larger society, the individual is willing to bear a certain level of anxiety, which instigates him to strive for the prestige of the approved relationship. With regard to upward status-mobility, in the sense of climbing the "democratic ladder," furthermore, this anxiety motivation is entirely realistic and rational in our kind of society. It is experienced both as an urge to flee from the deprivations of low status and as a pull toward the greater biological and social security of high-status persons.

In order to understand the prestige motivation of individuals of middle status, one must remember the severe social and biological punishments associated with low status. The anxiety which middle-status people learn is effective, first, because it involves the threat of loss of present status, and, secondly, because it leads, as the individual may plainly see in "successful" persons, to the rewards of power, of social prestige, and of security for one's children.

VII

There is a growing feeling in America that the competition for professional status is becoming more severe and that our status system generally is tightening. No doubt this belief contributes to the pressure for acceleration by our schools. Parents, as well as teachers and administrators, exert increasingly strong pressure upon the child from the time he is in elementary school. Middle-class parents, moreover, are increasingly fearful that their children will not qualify for admission to a "good" college. The tension builds up until the months preceding the announcement by colleges of their decisions upon applications; at that time even the best students often are in a nearly frenetic condition.

This whole process is a function of our social-class system. The social-class system in America is indeed becoming more sharply defined. But education is still the most readily available means of rising in the world. Even with education, however, an individual's upward mobility is slow; to climb one subclass in his lifetime, such as from lower-middle class to upper-middle class, constitutes an unusually rapid rate of social mobility for an individual.

Failure attends the efforts of the majority of those individuals who wish to rise to a higher status and actually attempt to do so. A major cause of these failures lies in the personalities of the individuals. In the following pages an effort will be made to define some of the personality factors related to success or failure in upward social movement. We have considered the relation of anxiety to status. Here the purpose is to examine the functions of aggression and of a sense of identity in facilitating the processes of upward status movement.

These processes usually begin in the early family life of the individual. Many parents seek to train their children toward upward mobility. Perhaps the prototype of such a parent is the immigrant who insists that all his children should become physicians, lawyers, or teachers, The son of such a father commented recently that everyone in his family had taken books seriously because his father considered the reading of English the most important factor in "getting up" in the American social system. In such a family, books have a kind of pragmatic value in addition to whatever value they may have as intellectual and imaginative stimuli. Books and school marks become "instruments" of social mobility. Although the ethnic cases may afford the more dramatic instances of the pushing and training of a child to rise above the status of his parents, it is of course true that many established American middle-class families train their children for extremely high goals, superior to those of the parents' occupational and educational standings.

Such parents really teach the child that he must be superior to his parents. To accomplish the Herculean task of becoming smarter and more successful than his own father or mother, the driven child apparently often learns to feel that he must actually be "perfect" in school and in work. Since he can never be perfect, he can never be satisfied with his success, no matter how great it may seem to others. Thus, to him, the game seems not worth the candle. For he can never extinguish his early learned need to be perfect, and therefore he must continue the pursuit of the ever retreating goal of perfection by driving himself toward increasingly greater attainment.

What of the parents who push their children hard and early for the attainment of the culture of a higher social level? Often such parents feel that they themselves have failed in the world. Their own hopes may have been blocked by lack of money or by undue economic responsibility for their own parents. The mother may feel that, as a woman, she has been prevented from achievement in business, law, medicine, or some other field dominated by men—an achievement which she deeply wanted. Such parents set the highest standards for their children, for they project their own ambitions upon the child. They feel that the child needs, more than anything else in life, the prestige and position in the world which the parents themselves always have desired.

Such a child may fail at upward mobility because he has been weakened, by parental guidance and pressure, in just those ego-functions which are essential for upward mobility. As a child, he learned from his parents that he could not direct his own life, stand on his own feet, make his own decisions both in the present and in the future. Although such children perform well in the academic world (a relatively simple world, where books are far more important than relationships with people), they often have trouble when they begin their careers. Their difficulty apparently results from their long-repressed hostility toward the parents, which is now displaced to other authority figures. It is likely that the child who believes he has not been allowed to make his own decisions will feel that he has been used and exploited, and the resultant hostility often will be transferred to his relationships with later authority figures. Such a child may also turn his (now guilty) resentment against himself and become self-punishing. In either case, whether by turning his resentment toward later parental figures, such as his boss, or by turning it inward against himself, he succeeds in being avenged upon the ambitious parent by failing in the world. Even "successful" individuals often are harried by feelings of unworthiness, of having betrayed their parents. Their guilt really may be due not to any actual failure but to their own resentment against their parents who drove them hard.

Another area in which the driven child may have difficulty as he grows up is that of relationships with the opposite sex. Where the mother has been the driver, the son may have difficulty, not only with objective authority figures, but also with women generally, including his wife, because he views women as authority figures like his mother.

Many parents who push their children toward social mobility are members of mixed-class marriages. The most common type of mixed-class marriage is that between a *woman from the lower-middle* class and a man from the top part of the working class. A lower-middle-class

woman who marries a man from the top
part of the working class usually begins
to try to recoup her original social-class
status either by reforming and elevating
her husband's behavior to meet lower-
middle-class standards or by seeking to
train and propel her children toward the
status which she once had or toward an
even higher status, thus compensating
for her "error." A similar situation may
arise with a man who has been downward mobile, due either to economic mis-
hap or to his having married into a lower
class. He may wish to help his children
to avoid the kind of error which he feels
he has made or the kind of deprivation
which he has had to undergo.

The child of such a mixed-class marriage faces many of the conflicts typical
of any marriage between individuals
from different cultures. He will be caught
between the lower-middle-class parent,
who will have the ideas of child-rearing,
the ambitions with respect to education,
and the concepts of sexual renunciation
which are typical of the lower-middle-
class culture, and the other parent from

the working class, who may have quite
different views with respect to education,
discipline, child-training goals, recreation, and sexual exploration. Thus the
conflict will be in the basic areas of life.
Such a conflict is most readily seen, however, in the area of education. The work-
ing-class father in such a mixed-class
marriage often feels that the girl or the
boy should go to work after she or he
had finished high school, but his wife
from the lower-middle class almost always feels that the child should go on to
college to train for a profession. This
conflict if often bitter; it is also pivotal,
since education is one of the most available means for upward mobility.

Until now this discussion has dealt
with children who have been "trained"
for mobility but trained, perhaps, in the
wrong way. The best training for upward mobility probably is training to be
independent, to make one's own decisions, to seek one's own goals, and to
have a proper degree and level of aggression. It is possible here to discuss only
aggression. The handling of aggression

—the control, direction, and transformation of his own aggression—is especially important for the successfully upward-mobile person. The basic means of controlling and redirecting aggression are learned in childhood and adolescence. Realistic social aggression is one of the child's basic ego functions. Aggression, in this sense, includes the initiative to defend oneself and to compete effectively in the areas of social and occupational attainment. It is one of the ego functions subsumed under the general concept of "autonomy." The type and level of aggression are largely a function of the individual's early relationships to his parents and siblings. The upward-mobile person comes out of his early family-life as a highly competitive individual. If he is to be successful in climbing, his aggression must be both realistically controlled and socially skillful.

The individual who has been socially, as distinguished from occupationally, upward-mobile proves to be one who has especially firm control of his hostility. The socially mobile individual has learned from childhood and adolescence not to fly in the face of authority. Instead, he has somehow learned to placate and win over the authority figures. He has not weighed himself down with fruitless and guilt-laden hostility or resentment toward the parent. With his parents, as later with his social-class superiors, he is a diplomat in aggression. He learns how far he may go, presses for his just due, but he also expects to knuckle under when necessary and is able to do so without losing his self-regard and without feeling undue humiliation and resentment.

As child and adult, such an individual has learned how to redirect and transform aggression into the socially approved virtues of competition and initiative. He has learned to walk the tightrope of his superiors' approval by skillful aggression (initiative), while avoiding defiance, on the one hand, and self-depreciation and guilt, on the other. This is his distinguishing characteristic, perhaps—this finely tempered aggression. He faces the constant, objective necessity to impress, and to win acceptance from, persons who have more power and more status than he has. These superiors must not, in spite of his efforts to enter their group, come to regard him as a "pusher" or as an *arriviste*. His must be an effective, but congenial and disarming, aggression.

VIII

The most difficult task faced by the upward-mobile child and adolescent is that of becoming identified with some group and of achieving a sense of personal identity. Erik Erikson has helped our understanding of adolescence by pointing out that the adolescent's central problem is the attainment of a sense of identity. To develop his identity, he must have a group, know what it is, and feel that he is intimately a part of it.

But the upward-mobile adolescent is leaving his family and group and therefore is losing his old identity. Moreover, his parents, if they are "ambitious for him," are urging and guiding the adolescent toward a culture and a social place which they themselves do not possess. Thus the adolescent in an upward-striving family is being directed toward an identity which neither he nor his parents can conceive in terms of those specific behaviors, goals, and values which the higher social status, or social class, demands; for the parents can define the identity goals of only that culture and that social class in which they have been participating. Thus the child or adolescent whose parents are consciously, or more often unconsciously, directing him toward a social class higher than their own cannot learn from his parents how to obtain recognition from this higher social class nor how to conceive of himself as a prospective member of the higher class. He is attempting to learn an identity without having the necessary targets for identification and without having a group which can give him, through mutual association and "recognition," the necessary help in conceiving or integrating his new ego-identity.

Thus, in upward-striving families, the adolescent is faced with two life-plans: that of his family's own culture and place and that of the more privileged culture and group which he is attempting to integrate into his life. The result is to intensify in these adolescents what Erikson calls "ego-diffusion."

Faced by two conflicting demands— (1) to follow the example and assume the identity of the parents or (2) to abandon much of the parents' culture and learn a culture to which neither they nor he has social access—the adolescent finds himself confronted by more social tasks, roles, and emotional problems than he can learn to handle. In this social situation and also, no doubt as a result of his deep-seated disappointment in the parents in earlier stages of his relationship to them, the adolescent may retreat to an identity which is the opposite of his parents'. Specifically he may move downward in his social-class participation, choosing radical groups, identifying with out-groups, marrying "out," or giving up the effort to form any identity at all.

On the other hand, those adolescents who have satisfactorily come through the earlier stages of development are capable of learning the identity of a higher social class and of eventually moving up into that class. But, in all probability, these successfully climbing individuals are precisely those who have not been dominated or had their life-plans mapped out by their parents.

IX

Status is one of the most difficult aspects of reality to accept. It is especially difficult for Americans to accept, owing to our having been taught that every man has the duty and the opportunity to improve his status. (In fact, however, not more than 20 per cent of Americans actually improve their class-status in their lifetime, and most of these are lower-middle-class persons who rise only one subclass.)

In the end, every child and man, even the socially mobile one, must accept the realities of some social status. Otherwise, he will play an escapist, neurotic game with a force which cannot be dreamed away or reasoned away. And he will have a weak sense of identity, a deep doubt as to who he is. This does not mean that a realist cannot also "rise in the world." The person who succeeds at upward mobility is a realist concerning status. He has identified successfully with a higher status-group, and he has learned sufficient control of his hostility so that he can be cooperative with people of higher status.

He also has identified with the culture of a higher social class. He has sought to take this new culture into himself because he admires it and considers it superior to the culture of his own parents. This process of incorporating the values and behavior of the superior, envied, and admired higher status-group is the basic psychological process in upward social mobility and in acculturation. The process may begin with the individual's defensive "identification with the aggressor," but it does not end there. For it results in the learning of a new culture within which he can exercise his initiative and special competencies more effectively.

Identification with the culture of a higher social group, that is, the belief that their culture is more intelligent and more refined, helps to reduce the striving individual's fear of, and hostility toward, that group. But it is only when the upward-striving individual attains the status, itself, and participates in it, that his

hostility and anxiety are effectively reduced and his sense of new identity confirmed by his new status-group.

But even in this new higher status, he
always will find that there are individuals or groups of still higher status. So,
he always must learn to reconcile his
desires, cravings, and drives to those of
individuals who have greater social prestige and authority than he has; that is, he
must learn, if he wishes to reduce his
anxiety and hostility to a tolerable level.

When one considers that psycho-social
development in the United States consists of learning the culture and sanctions of a succession of ranked statuses
— in childhood, in the school, in the
armed services, in industry, in parenthood, in old age—our society and its culture do not appear nearly so "discontinu-
ous" as Ruth Benedict and others have
thought them to be. Through each of
these status-relationships, whether of
father to son, mother to daughter, older
brother to younger brother, teacher to
pupil, peer-group leader to follower, offi-
cer to enlisted man, or employer to work-

er, there runs a cultural and psychological continuity. It results in part, from the status-structure of our society and of all other Western societies. This continuity is the basically similar socio-psychological processes involved in the various types of status-relationships.

With respect to both authority-relationships, and also to movement upward from one class to another, our society can operate efficiently only if it encourages some degree of change in authority- and status-relationships. That is, our status-systems of age, class, and ethnic groups provide cultural controls not only for maintaining these status-groups but also for *recruiting individuals from one age, class, or ethnic group into a higher status*.

Our society has continuity, therefore, both in the sense of (a) *stability* (the status-structures) and also of (b) *socially controlled change through time* (movement through various age-statuses, and individual recruitment from one class to another).

It seems true that the parent-child relationship is the prototype from which all other relationships of *authority* are learned. And the sibling-relationships and age-group constitute the basic psycho-social situations in which *competition* and social aggression are learned and from which they are displaced to the social class and ethnic competitiveness necessary for social mobility. The relative ease or difficulty of an individual's relationships to persons in authority—as well as to his peers—in any status-system are probably greatly influenced by the degree to which he has solved his feelings toward his parents and his sibling-rivalrous feelings in childhood and adolescence. If he has achieved a reconciliation to the parent of the same sex and if he has at length, after normal sibling-rivalry, become reconciled to his brothers and sisters, he seems likely to advance to other good status-relationships both with authority-figures and with his social equals.

Within each status-identity, he may exercise the ego-functions of relative self-direction, initiative, and competence and also enjoy approval by, and social intimacy with, a group of his own. In each successive status he has to learn to act efficiently, to exercise initiative, to achieve, but within the cultural limits set by the society for that status. To put it differently, the ego of every normal individual achieves a certain relative autonomy, but, if the anxiety and hostility connected with this degree of autonomy are to be kept within normal limits, the individual must reconcile himself emotionally to the objective social sanctions of age-status, sex-status, and the other basic types of social status.